GOAL !

A Soccer Handbook for Young Players

by: Paul E. Harris, Jr.

Illustrated by: Ralph Ford

Cover Design: *Jackie and John Shanahan*

Cover Photo: *Robert Silberling*

SOCCER FOR AMERICANS
Box 836
Manhattan Beach, Calif., 90266

Library of Congress Catalog Number: 76-5333
ISBN 0-916802-01-9

SOCCER FOR AMERICANS
Box 836
Manhattan Beach, Calif. 90266

The author with his wife, Doris, Julie (right), Pablo, and Michelle. The dogs are named Inky and Perkins.

Paul E. Harris, Jr. (right, at the age of 3, when he first discovered soccer).

Paul E. Harris Jr., the author of GOAL! has enjoyed soccer for more than 30 years. He has "reffed" almost 1000 games, and is always trying to interest young people in soccer. "The thing I like most is seeing people having a good time at soccer", he says. He lives in Manhattan Beach, California with his wife and three children.

Ralph Ford (left) is the illustrator for GOAL!. Samuel Shinguard, and other characters, have delighted his fifth grade students at Robinson School, in Manhattan Beach, California. He lives with his wife Sara, and daughter Rebecca in Manhattan Beach.

Goal! is dedicated to all young soccer players everywhere!

photo by Gabor Lovy

GOAL!

A Soccer Handbook for Young Players

TABLE OF CONTENTS

The soccer ball. It brings people together everywhere, all over the world. This is the ball used in the North American Soccer League. (Photo courtesy North American Soccer League)

1
THE WORLD OF SOCCER

Many boys and girls (and parents) dream of getting aboard a huge tanker or steamship to sail the high seas. They think of stopping in an occasional port for rest and relaxation, then going on to another destination. If you were to take such a trip, and bring your soccer ball with you, within minutes after stepping on land you would find a friend to share your interest. Whether you stopped in Plymouth, England, Padang on the island of Sumatra or Beira at the north end of Mozambique, you would find that many people of all ages know and love the game you are now playing.

Soccer at home here in the United States is fairly new for young people, but it has grown. Countless thousands of players now compete in all 50 of our states. The game has grown in popularity mainly because it is fun. When you walk off a soccer field, you know you've been in an active, safe game, where everyone has had plenty of chances to play. And, if you have ever experienced the explosion of excitement that follows a goal, you know what joys the game brings.

Soccer brings people together as a team, yet the game allows you to be an individual and to develop ways of stopping, passing, and kicking the ball. And, you don't have to be a giant, a speedy runner, or a "muscle man" to play. All you need is some interest and a willingness to practice. Once you get started in soccer, you won't want to stop. Read the book carefully, and pay attention to what Samuel J. Shinguard has to say. He's been playing soccer for quite a while now, and he knows what its all about.

Samuel J. Shinguard (above) was named by Sean Garrity of Robinson School in Manhattan Beach, California.

WHAT MADE PELE PERHAPS THE GREATEST PLAYER EVER TO KICK A SOCCER BALL?

1. His superior condition. He worked hard to stay in shape.

2. His natural ability and build. He had extraordinary coordination and physique.

3. His attitude toward soccer. He loved the game, and put everything he had into it. He still does.

4. His ability to foresee things on the field. It is said that Pele knew what an opponent would do before he did it.

5. His attitude toward himself. He never let a missed shot get him down.

6. His attitude toward his teammates. He never kept the ball to himself when someone else was open. Most people remember him for his 1200 goals. He many many assists, too, and made chances for teammates.

7. His willingness to practice. Pele knew that even the easiest of moves needed to be repeated over and over.

8. His timing. Whether he was up to head a ball or getting ready for a volley, he seldom misplayed a ball.

9. His variety of moves. When he had the ball and came to an opponent, he had many choices for what to do.

10. His awareness of what was going on around him. Pele knew where his teammates and the opponents were.

Sometimes players bunch up around the goal. How many players can you count in this picture? Some of them should not be there. (Photo by Don Lesher)

4

WHAT REALLY HAPPENS IN YOUR SOCCER GAME?

When you ask a friend what happened in their game, you will probably get the answer, "We won, 2-1", or "they really whipped us, 5-2." Young players seldom think very hard about why they won, or lost, or about what really went on during play.

If you've played at all, you know that any time there's a penalty kick, someone made a mistake. Who knows, it may even be the Referee! But did you know that *each* time a goal is scored, someone has made a mistake? The perfect soccer game has never been played. It is possible to have a perfect game in bowling, or archery, but not in soccer. There are too many chances for error.

When a forward breaks through and scores, someone wasn't playing him close enough, and allowed him too much space. Or, when a player dribbles down the sideline, someone should have tackled him. But don't let this bother you. Everyone makes mistakes, as hundreds of moves are made in each game. The team that wins, unless it is very lucky, will make fewer mistakes. All players should play the game with the idea of making fewer errors.

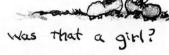

Was that a girl?

Back to what happens in your games:

1. Less than one of three passes you make will go where you want it.

2. You will only touch the ball about 35 times each game. When you do, it usually doesn't do what you want it to do.

3. 300 passes will be made each game. If a team makes 3 good passes in a row, that's considered excellent. If that happens often, you are probably on a championship team. Think of it!

4. If your team takes more than 15 good shots at goal during a game, they are also headed for the championship. Most shots are taken inside the penalty area.

5. What you do when you do not have the ball will determine how often you get the ball.

Some of this may sound discouraging, but you should understand that soccer is a game demanding skills that are practiced over and over. The best players are usually those who have practiced the hardest and longest. You must work all the time with the skills of the game, make fewer and fewer mistakes as you become experienced, and encourage your teammates to do the same.

Whatever happens in your game, indoors or out, there will be action. (Photo by Ed Fosmire)

If you want to become a better player, you'll have to practice your skills. (Photo by Gary Weaver)

3
THE SKILLS OF SOCCER

As in any sport, anything you can do is easy, and anything you cannot do is difficult. This chapter is to help you learn what you'll be doing most in soccer. Start with a few easy things. Then you'll want to work on harder things later.

Throughout this book you will find words and advice about practice, ball, control, and the development of your skills. These terms are all the same, and they add up to what you will need most in soccer — control over the ball.

Since the ball is usually pushed, stopped, or delayed in flight by the use of the feet, and since soccer is a game played almost entirely with the feet, ball juggling with the feet should be your most important exercise. You can juggle the ball alone, and without an audience, knowing that with practice you will soon be able to keep the ball in the air for two or three kicks. Now try with your weak foot. The hopping, or juggling, movement will develop your coordination, and the act of getting the ball in the air without touching it with the hands is quite an accomplishment!

Later on, use your thighs, chest, head, anything except but the hands to keep it going. Don't become discouraged, for every time you come in contact with the ball you'll be getting better. And, juggling is not for show-offs. It is excellent for beginning your practice, for warming up, and for getting used to your whole body as you master the ball. The ball will be part of you, but only if you become a part of it, starting today.

Kicking

The most popular kick, though not the one you should use most often, is the **instep** kick. The instep is that hard, arched part of your foot that is covered by your shoelaces. Before you can kick with the instep, remember the position of the non-kicking leg. It should be alongside the ball, slightly bent, 6 inches away from the ball, with the toes pointed in the direction you want the ball to go. Curl the toes down on your kicking foot, and follow through. Try it in slow motion first. This instep kick is the hard kick you will use for scoring goals and for making long passes.

The skill you will use more than any other is the easiest, but only if you practice it regularly. This is the kick with the *inside* of the foot. Most contacts with the ball are made with this 7 inch part of your shoe. They can be made very accurate, and with almost no effort. Again, the support foot points in the direction you are to be kicking. Start in slow motion, and follow-through is even more important

Dribbling

Dribbling is the art of "earning extra room" on the field, while running with the ball under control. Clever dribbling often brings cheers from the sidelines, but something must be accomplished by it. Too much dribbling slows the game, brings on fights for the ball, and wears you out. A successful dribble should gain you the extra room you need for a pass or shot on goal. Otherwise, your dribble has been worthless.

10

It is best to first practice with your strong kicking foot, using the front of the foot, on either side of the toes. The touch is made just below the center of the ball.

Dribbling should be a part of your daily routine as you become familiar with the soccer ball. Try it walking, running, jogging, always keeping the ball within reach. Pretend that it is tied to an elastic that will not stretch more than one yard in front of you.

Keep your head up and know where you are going, always looking for someone who is open! Don't make the mistake many young players do, by always watching the ball when you dribble.

Heading

More than any other move in the game, heading brings the comment from someone who has not played the game, "Doesn't that hurt?" The answer is, "Yes, if you don't know how to do it."

Before you worry about those balls in the air that seem to be aimed at your head, take a ball in your hands and strike it against the center of your forehead. This will locate the right spot and increase your confidence.

Now that you know where the ball is to strike your head, have someone throw you a few to "head". Hold your arms out for balance. After this have the ball thrown high so you'll have to jump for it. Remember to keep your eyes open and mouth closed. As soon as you're no longer afraid of the ball, you'll want to learn how to use your whole body to "snap" the ball with your head. There is no one, including the goalie, who shouldn't be a good "header" on the team. Do it right, and there will be no headaches.

Tackling

Except for intercepting a ball in the air or on the ground tackling is the most common way of getting the ball away from the opponent. It is done only with the feet. The tackling foot is always turned sideways, with the body leaning forward. The non-tackling foot is close in, so the ball will not "squirt" away.

Tackle the ball, not the player, and do it with the feet.

Although it has been said that soccer is not a contact game, the tackle brings most of the allowed contact that occurs in the game. No other move requires more of your strength and desire to get the ball.

Occasionally you will be in a bad position for a tackle, yet in need of kicking the ball away. A sliding tackle is legal. Unlike most tackles, you don't want possession. Pretend you're sliding into third base, except that you want to jar the bag loose! Slide-tackle *only* if you have to.

TRAPPING THE BALL

Trapping is the most fundamental of all the skills in soccer. If you want to trap an animal you offer bait; in soccer if you want to trap a ball you must offer part of your body as a cushion. The part of the body you use depends on the height of the ball when it reaches you. Most balls which come your way can be handled with the foot or leg.

Foot traps

The sole of the foot trap is easy. Stretch your receiving leg out, with the heel about 4-6 inches from the ground, with the toe pointed up. Pull the leg back toward you (slightly), as contact is made. This will bring the ball to you, and right at your feet.

When you use the inside-of-the-foot trap, your non-trapping foot is pointed toward the ball. Use the large flat portion of your foot to receive the ball. Keep the foot 2-3 inches off the ground to keep the ball from going over the foot. Do it in slow motion first.

14

The outside-of-the-foot trap looks harder than it is, and many players don't even try it. Use that part of the boot just below and ahead of the ankle. This move gives you extra time for that next move, for you don't have to make the awkward turn to use the inside. This is good for balls that are hit at a medium speed toward you.

Completing the use of the foot in trapping is the instep, normally used only for hard kicking. The instep trap is not easy, but is worth trying. Catch the ball on your instep. Juggling the ball will help you with this.

BODY TRAPS

If you do not have room or time to use your feet in a trap, you will sometimes have to use your chest or thigh. Once you have confidence in using your feet for controlling the ball, you will want to experiment with the many ways of stopping the ball and keeping it at your feet. Always remember that when the ball is coming toward you it should be thought of as a very fragile egg. Treat it gently and it will stay with you and not escape to an opponent.

Volleying

As in tennis, volleying is meeting the ball before it reaches the ground. It is done when you don't have the room or the time to trap the ball. The most accurate way to volley a ball is with the side of the foot. Once you are good at this, you may want to try volleying with the instep. The instep volley is for harder and longer kicks.

The half-volley occurs when you kick a ball on the short hop, like a drop-kick. Sometimes goalies like to half-volley the ball out of their hands.

Sam Shinguard is sometimes forgetful. He forgot to show you the points on his shoe that he uses for dribbling.

Meet Adrian Walsh of Galway, Ireland. He has set the World Record for juggling a soccer ball. On November 5th, 1975, Adrian kept the ball in the air for 80 minutes, and he touched the ball 8,700 times! (Photo by Oto Maximilian)

*The rules allow for the goalkeeper to put the ball back
into play without interference. (Photo by Fred Rasmussen)*

4
IMPROVING THROUGH KNOWING THE LAWS

Soccer is played everywhere under the same basic set of rules. The 17 "Laws of the Game" have changed very little over the years. If you are going to be playing in an organized league, the ball may be somewhat smaller than regulation and the game probably less than the full 90 minutes. Otherwise, the rules of soccer apply for you as they do for the other millions of players on the five continents. Fifteen of the 17 rules are listed briefly here, with some hints for you. Two of the rules are discussed in more detail.

Law 1. The Field of Play
(see illustration) Fields must never be square, but sometimes they are quite long.

Hints:
a. Look over the field before you play, and check for soft spots, holes, and drains. It might save you an injury.
b. Study the illustration, know the markings and what they are for. See "The Language of Soccer" at the end of the book for terms.

Law 2. The Ball
Maximum sized balls are 27-28 inches around, and weigh between 14 and 16 ounces.

Hints:
a. It makes sense to practice with the size ball you will use in your games.

b. If you are a goalie, make sure you feel the game ball before starting play. Don't let its size and weight surprise you.

Law 3. Number of Players

The game is played with eleven players, including the goalie. A substitute may enter the field only when the Referee allows him to, and a player who has been "ordered off" may not be replaced.

Law 4. Players Equipment

Cleats can be made of rubber, plastic, aluminum, leather, or similar material. Nothing can be worn which is considered dangerous to another player. The goalie's shirt must be different from all the other players and from the Referee's.

Law 5. Referees

The Referee is in charge of the game. He has control from the time he enters the field until the time he leaves, including before kickoff at halftime and when he leaves after the game is over.

Hints:
a. Remember the "advantage". (see language of soccer again.) If you have been fouled, but the team has not lost the ball, the "Ref"

may decide not to blow his whistle.

b.   Good players never have problems with referees. They are too busy playing the game.

c.   No referee tries to cheat you. Sometimes it just seems that way.

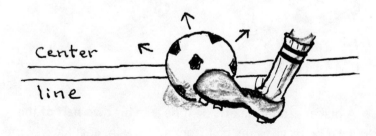

Law 6. Linesmen

They signal balls out of play and call offsides by using a flag.

Hint: Don't worry if you think that someone else last touched the ball, but you don't get the throw-in. You'll get the ball right away, anyway.

Law 7. Duration of the Game

In adult soccer, two periods of 45 minutes each. Your games will be shorter, according to league rules.

Hint: Don't ask the Referee how much time is left in your game. He's not required to tell you.

Law 8. The Start of Play

The game is started at midfield at the beginning of the game, after a goal is scored, and after halftime. The ball must be kicked forward, and must travel its circumference before it can be played again.

Center

line

Law 9. Ball In and Out of Play

The ball is out of play when it has crossed the touch line or goal line, in the air or on the ground, or when the game has been stopped by the Referee. It is in play at all other times.

>   **Hint:** Play the whistle. If it doesn't sound, keep playing.

Law 10. Method of Scoring

For a goal to be good, the ball must be over the goal line between the posts, and under the crossbar. The goalie's feet or body have nothing to do with it.

Law 11. Offside

A player should not be ahead of the ball when the ball is played in his direction unless he has two opponents ahead of him.

A player cannot be offside if he is in his own half of the field, or if he receives the ball from a throw-in, goal kick, corner kick, or drop ball. If a player from the other team plays it to you, you cannot be offside.

Hints:

a. Don't worry too much about this law! Play the game and you will soon learn about the law. Just try to keep two opponents between you and their goal.

b. A forward player who is never called for offsides is not playing close enough to the defense.

If you have any questions about the offside, ask your coach, or ask the Referee at halftime or before the game. Fourteen year old Peter Wildharbor explains the offside law to a young player. (Photo by John Ferrer)

Law 12. Fouls and Misconduct

This law guides the fair conduct of the game, and shows which actions are not allowed. Everything not defined here is allowed, and fair. The nine offenses listed here all must be judged INTENTIONAL, and result in a **direct free kick.**
(the ball can go directly in goal)

Kicking or attempting to kick

Tripping

Jumping at an opponent

Charging from behind, unless the opponent is obstructing

Charging in a violent or dangerous manner

Striking or attempting to strike

Holding

Pushing

Handling the ball

24

These five offenses are penalized by an **indirect free kick.**
(the ball must be touched by another player from either team
before going into goal)

1.   *Playing dangerously.*

2.   *Charging fairly, but when the ball
     is not in playing distance.*

3.   *Obstructing an opponent.*

4.   *Charging the goalkeeper.*

5.   *When playing goalie, taking more
     than four steps, or wasting time.*

The rest of the law deals with the conduct of the players toward themselves, the spectators, and the Referee. Unless a player is guilty of violent conduct, serious foul play, or if he uses foul or abusive language, he is given a "second chance" by the Referee. The "second chance" is a yellow card (caution). The serious things which the player must not repeat are:

a. Entering or leaving the field without the Referee's permission.
b. Disagreeing with the Referee.
c. Being guilty of unsportsmanlike conduct.

Hints:

a. The captain has no special rights with the Referee. The Referee may want to talk with the captain, but usually the Referee won't listen to any advice.
b. Fouls lead to misconduct. Players who play within the laws are never cautioned, or ejected.

Law 13. Free Kicks

As you noticed in Law 12, there are two kinds of free kicks. The Referee raises his arm before an indirect kick is taken. All other kicks are direct. For any kick to be good,

a. The ball must be placed at the point of the infraction,
b. The ball must not be rolling, and
c. It must travel its circumference before it is considered "in play."

Hints:

a. Defensive players must retreat 10 yards when a kick has been awarded.
b. Take most free kicks as soon as you can. This will surprise your opponents.

Law 14. Penalty Kick

A Penalty kick is taken from the penalty spot (12 yards from goal) when one of the nine fouls (see law 12) is committed inside the penalty area. When the kick is taken, all players except the goalie and the kicker must be outside of the penalty area and penalty arc.

Law 15. Throw-In

The ball is thrown in from the touch line (side line) where it left the field. The thrower must be facing the field, and have part of each foot either on the line or behind it, and the ball is to be thrown from behind and over the head with both hands.

Hint: Throwing the ball in is easy. You can learn how to do it right in one minute. Do it immediately in a game. Don't wait!

Law 16. Goal Kicks

If the attacking team last touches a ball before it goes over the goal line, the defensive team takes a goal kick. The kick is taken from within the goal area.

Hints:
a. The best place for goal kicks is at the top of the goal area. It does not have to be in the corner of the goal area.
b. The goalie should take goal kicks, if at all possible.

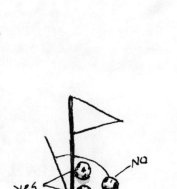

Law 17. Corner Kicks

If the defensive team last touched the ball, over the goal line, the attacking team takes a corner kick from the closer corner. These kicks are taken from within the corner circle.

This player, Soren Banks, is showing perfect form, and he is wearing his shinguards in case his opponent does not have perfect form! (Photo by Peter Alan Stone, D.D.S.)

5
WEAR THOSE SHINGUARDS
(SOME IDEAS ON EQUIPMENT)

Beginning soccer players should know that for practice all you really need is a ball. Whether you are going to practice alone or with your friends, in the rain or in the sun, on the beach or in the backyard, the ball is important, and you should have your own.

Make sure that the ball you get is not too big. An official ball is 28 inches around (maximum) and weighs 16 ounces (maximum). Unless you are 16 years old, this is too big. The ball should be the same number of ounces in weight as your age. If you are 12, a 12 or 13 ounce ball is just right. It should also be water-repellent (without stitching) so you won't have to worry about getting it wet. Later on you can buy a leather ball with stitching, but for now you should have a ball that you can play with in all conditions without worry about damage and wear. If you keep your ball deflated when you are not using it, the ball will stay with you even longer.

After you've decided you really like soccer and you're going to be on a team, you should have soccer shoes. The best ones for you have molded rubber cleats and a padded tongue over the instep. Make sure you have room for the extra pair of socks and that the shoes fit comfortably. With your normal growth, if you buy shoes a little big, they will last you two seasons.

When you play on a team, you will probably be given a shirt, socks, and shorts. These are to be worn only on game days. For practice, wear clothes that are comfortable, and avoid long pants for scrimmages. Don't bundle up too much for practice. Soccer is a game of movement, and you must be able to practice the great moves you'll make in games.

Finally, always wear a pair of shinguards. Don't be impressed by older players who leave shinguards in the locker room. Sooner or later someone will miss the ball and kick your shin, usually down near the ankle. Shinguards are sensible, and not for sissies! Wear them all the time and you'll never know they're on.

6
TEAMMATES
EACH ONE IS DIFFERENT

The Pele film showed a great player in practice, something very few people have seen. He is shown with his teammates, and they are all working for one thing . . . improvement! Pele's teammates were not as well known as he, but they all worked together to improve themselves and the team. Their secret was learning from each other, and each one is certainly different.

You may think that you are the strongest (or weakest) player on your team, but you probably are neither. Whatever your strong or your weak points, there are certain things that you can do to prove you are part of a TEAM game.

1. Support the efforts of each player. No player tries to miss a goal or a tackle. "Nice try" is always good to hear.

2. Do a lot of helpful talking on the field. Let teammates know you are there. Silence is for tennis and chess.

3. Calling for the ball when you are open is different than yelling for it when the ball cannot possibly be passed. Make your voice mean something.

4. If someone on your team scores a goal, go over and give a handshake and a congratulation. If you score, go over to the player who made the pass to you. You couldn't have made the goal without help!

5. If you blame someone for a mistake, it will probably happen again. If you try to understand and support the player, he will do better. Remember, the next mistake may be yours!

6. The best thing you can do for your teammates is to try. Go to every practice, listen to your coach, and show that you are doing your best.

*Teammates sometimes get too close together. (Photo
by Bob Silberling)*

The coach, Dan McKinnon, and his two players, are happy.
They just won a state championship. (Photo courtesy of
Dan McKinnon)

34

7
YOUR COACH

SOCCER is new to many American players. You may be surprised to find that when you go to your first practice, the game is new to your coach, too. Don't let this bother you. The youth coach you see on the opposite page had a championship team his first year, and is now one of the most successful coaches in America. In many places, the game is being played, coached, and officiated by newcomers. If your coach is new, you might tell him about some of the materials listed in the back of this book.

Whether your coach is young or old, new or experienced, male or female, remember that there are 15 players or more to work with, and that everyone deserves a chance. If you think you are one of the better players, you will have many chances to help the others. Soccer is a team game, and depends on everyone helping the coach.

Hints:
1. Always be to practice early, and properly dressed.
2. Never talk to or distract others when the coach is talking.
3. Never question the coach's decisions. If something bothers you about what the coach is doing, talk it over with him after practice or with some-

one at home, or with a friend. They may
help you understand.

4.   Try to set an example for others to follow.

5.   Be willing to try new positions on the team.

Coaches learn by playing, too. (Photo by Don Rogers)

These players have both been well-coached. They are using a fair shoulder charge when the ball is within playing distance. (Photo by Bill Kerylow)

Pele, even at the age of 18, knew that he could be a better player if he understood how goalkeepers play. (Courtesy, Domicion Pinhero and Pepsi-Cola)

8
GOALKEEPERS AND GOALSCORERS
LETS HAVE MORE OF THEM

The play that creates the most excitement in soccer centers around the goal. The strikers and other forwards move toward the goal and take shots, with the goalkeeper and defenders trying everything to stop them. Why is it that, with everyone intent on scoring, that more goals are not scored? Here are some of the reasons:

1. Some players would rather not take a chance on missing.

Hint: Even the greatest player made only one goal in ten attempts. Don't worry about missing. Your teammates will encourage your try.

2. Players feel they cannot score unless they are close to the goal.

Hint: In the goalie's eyes, you are always very close. When you are in the penalty area, shoot! If you are close enough to have the ball at your feet, shoot toward the goal. There is no such thing as a ball hog in the penalty area.

3. Players look around too much when they have the ball in the penalty area.

Hint: This is one time when you should not look up and search for teammates or for space. Don't worry about searching for the goal, as it is plenty big enough.

4. The strong kicking foot is favored.

Hint: If you can use only one foot, you are limiting your chances. In practice, take most of your shots with the weak foot. It will become stronger.

5. Players seldom practice scoring. They just practice kicking at a goal.

Hint: When you practice shooting, do it with a teammate. Have him kick the ball toward you. Wait until he is close, then shoot or dribble around him. Get used to shooting under pressure. Keep moving when near goal, always searching for that opening.

6. Players stand and watch the shots go toward the goal.

Hint: Follow up on every shot, as you will get many rebound shots off the post or from players. When the ball is headed toward the goal, move in toward the goal, not toward the ball!

7. Players worry about being called offsides.

Hint: A good forward is whistled for offsides at least once a game. That usually means he is playing close to the fullback.

8. Players wait before putting the ball in play.

Hint: Soccer is a game of quick starts, and surprises. If you get a throw-in or a free kick, take it quickly. You will always surprise someone, and sometimes everyone.

9. Passes and kicks are not varied.

Hints: Most passes and shots are best made on the ground, with the side of the foot. Harder and longer shots are made with the instep. Learn to do each one quickly. Don't let the other team guess what you're going to do.

10. Players give up on balls they think they cannot get.

Hint: Be aggressive. There is nothing that worries the other player more then someone who is determined to get the ball.

If you remember just one or two of these hints, you will score more goals and enjoy the game more. You will also do what few players can accomplish — put the ball in the net, where it belongs.

Now that you think you know a little about goal scoring, take a turn in goal. Read the chapter on goalkeeping, the position where the most dependable team player should play. The more you learn about goalkeeping, the more you will learn about what it takes to be an effective goalscorer.

Fifteen years later, Pele still takes a turn in goal.
(Courtesy Domicion Pinhero and Pepsi-Cola)

Some players act as if they really don't like to play in goal. Do you think this player likes his position? (Photo by Don Rogers)

Players who take practice seriously will do better in the game. (Photo by Gary Weaver)

9

LETS HAVE A LEFT FOOTED GAME

If you have seen Pele in the film "The Master and His Method", you probably came away with many ideas on how to improve your soccer. This film tells and shows you so much, but in a simple way. So it is with the game, a collection of simple moves by players, all meant to beat an opponent.

There are no shortcuts to success in soccer, and Pele would be the first to tell you. The skills you acquire will depend almost entirely on the time you spend with the ball in **practice**.

Practicing Alone

Soccer provides you with many chances to practice when you are bored, and looking for things to do. You need only a small space and a ball.

1. The most important skill is jug-gling, the best way for you to warm up and begin your practice.
2. Practice kicking the ball against a wall. If you get close enough to the wall, you can practice the volley with the instep. Get closer yet and you can work on "head-ing". Keep the ball moving and

don't worry about "still" balls for you won't get many of them in a game. Shoot hard against the wall for accuracy and strength. Trap the ball when it returns.

3. A tether ball on the end of a four foot rope develops coordination and confidence. Or, anchor a longer rope to the ground and practice kicking with the instep or side of the foot. You'll get lots of kicks, and no chasing of the ball. A good chance to use that weak foot, now that no one is watching.

4. Use a small ball like a tennis ball for dribbling. Watch your control improve.

5. Run hard with the ball at your feet from a standstill position. This is called acceleration. It's not how fast you run in soccer that really counts, it's how fast you start. Begin every run with a fake so you can outmaneuver your opponent. One good fake is stepping over the ball, or pretending to, with either foot.

6. Use the tether ball again and hang it from a tree limb, high enough so you have to jump to head it. Now hang it six inches off the ground and kick it. Use that instep for your hard kicks.

7. Pass the ball from the inside of one foot to the inside of the other, keeping the ball moving. This develops "ball awareness."

8. Place your foot on top of the ball, and pull it back toward you. This will give you extra

room to pass or to dribble, if the opponent
is too close.

Practicing with Others

If you're lucky, you'll have a coach who knows a lot of
ways of making your practice sessions interesting. After all,
scrimmages do get tiring, and you also learn a lot in smaller
games. You and your coach should know what all experienced
coaches and players know: the fewer players in a group, the
more time each player will have with the ball. Also, no one
should stand around with nothing to do. Four or five players
is the ideal number to have for most group games. The kind
of game you play depends on which skill you want to develop.
Here are a few:

1. Keeping the Ball. Three against two. Four
    passes by the three players without losing the
    ball counts as a goal.

2. Looking for the Open Player. Three against
    two. There should always be an "open man"
    for the three-player team, and this is achieved
    by all three moving. This develops aggressive-
    ness for the team of two players.

3. Quick Thinking and Passing. Each of four
    players has a number. The player with the ball
    shouts a number. The numbered player shouts,
    "my number", and he must then receive the
    quick pass. A fifth player could be in the
    middle to intercept. If he gets to the numbered
    player first, another number is shouted.

4. Throwing-In and Heading. Three players. One
    throws the ball to the other, who is guarded from
    behind. The receiver heads or volleys it back to
    the feet of the thrower.

5. Using Different Passes. Four against one. The player in the middle shouts the kind of pass to be used, and must try to get the ball away. The passes to be used can be toe-pass, heel-pass, inside-of-foot-pass, instep-pass, and outside-of-the-foot-pass.

6. Tackling. Two players are facing each other, and are an equal distance from the ball. At a signal they must run for the ball, and tackle it away from the opponent.

7. Quick Passing. Three against three, in a small space. Players can only touch the ball twice, once to trap it and once to pass. Now try without trapping, as in "one touch".

8. Marking. One against two. One player is to stay very close to his opponent, who must break loose to receive a pass from a team-mate. The kicker will learn to pass to an open space.

9. Conditioning. Four on each side on a half-sized field. No offsides, no goalie. The ball has to pass over the goal line for a goal. Play nonstop for 8 minutes.

10. Teamwork. Now try the same eight players in a small space, like 15 yards square. You'll have to get rid of the ball quickly, for you don't have much room. Two short passes are always better than one long one.

11. Looking for the Open Player. Five against six. There should always be an open player for one team. Play in slow motion by "walking" through this game. You'll then have more success in looking for the open player.

12. Developing the Instep. Groups of two players stand 10 yards apart, kicking the ball out of their hands on the instep (volley). The partner catches or traps it and kicks the ball back the same way. Move back two steps after each. kick until you are 20 yards apart.

13. Confidence in heading and practice in kicking to the goal. One player is in the goal, and one ten yards away with five balls. The player in goal is to "head" out all shots by the kicker. Each shot is to be sent three or four feet off the ground. Don't retrieve balls until all five have been kicked.

14. Kicking for accuracy. Kick rolling balls at a small goal or at targets 15, 30, and 45 feet away. Targets can be two cones three yards apart.

15. Dribbling for speed. Have a dribbling relay race around five cones, five feet apart. You'll have to keep the ball close to you.

16. Heading. Two or three players stand on each side of the goal, and practice heading the ball over the top. Use feet for "volley" kicks, but don't let the ball touch the ground. If you do this twice in a row, that's very good.

17. Forming Pairs. Five players against three. In these games, never more than 10 minutes long, you should learn to form "pairs" of players. Each player on the team of five should always have a player nearby ready for a pass.

18. Trapping and Passing. Four players stand at the four corners of an 8 yard square. Keep balls moving around the square, passing with

left foot, trapping with right. No hurry about this. Look up before each pass reaches you, pretending to look for an open player. If you develop the habit of looking around before you receive a ball, you'll know when to pass.

19. Kicking Good and Bad Balls. Stand at the 18 yard line. Have someone kick balls in your direction, some from the side, some from in front. Don't trap them. Kick right at the goal without waiting. Get used to kicking "bad" balls. That's the way they come to you in the game. If one in five goes into the goal, even without a goalkeeper, you're doing all right.

20. Passing for Accuracy. Two players are 5 yards apart. A third player is standing midway between them, with legs spread apart. The two players pass the ball through his legs. First they trap the ball and shoot. Later they pass the rolling ball without waiting. Change positions when you miss, and keep score.

21. Going for The Goal. A goalie stands in goal, with a player on the 18 yard line. Someone rolls a ball midway between them. The goalie must dive on the ball or kick it away. The kicker must send it into the goal. Balls can be thrown in the air for "headers".

22. For Reaction While Dribbling. Two players, each with a ball. One dribbles around the field, and the other follows in his steps, like a "copy-cat".

23. For Dribbling and Control. Seven players are inside a large circle, each with a ball. Five other players each try to get a ball away from one of the seven. When the ball is taken away, the new player dribbles. Always try to keep the body between the ball and the opponent.

24. For Conditioning and Aggressiveness. Two opposing players on a 40 yard long field, with one goalie in each goal. Each of the two opposing players tries to score in the opponent's goal. Each of these games should last no more than two minutes, for there is constant running. Good for goalies, too.

25. For Reaction and Conditioning. Place a cone or other marker on the 18 yard (penalty area) line. Stand on the goal line between the posts and run to the marker. When you have almost arrived at the marker, have someone kick a ball in your direction. Kick it at goal while running back. Do this five times in a row, without stopping.

There are many games you can play. They should all be played to improve your physical condition and skill. Now, try to invent some games of your own. When it comes to improving, soccer is like all other sports. You must practice a little each day. When you do, the ball will begin to work for you. There is no greater joy in soccer!

51

Playing goalie is fun, even though no one pays attention to you until the ball comes. (Photo by Bob Silberling)

52

10
ME, A GOALIE?

Most young players want to play goalie all of the time or not at all. Each attitude is wrong. Everyone should get a chance to see what it is like. It will make you a better player to know how the field looks from the goalie's position, and it might just help you score more goals! If you really want to be only a goalie, you will have to use your feet as well, so practice out in the field with your team.

Playing goalie is not easy, especially after someone has just scored a goal against you and everyone is looking at you and at the ball in the net. Many goalies are unsure of themselves, and are especially afraid to come out for high balls. Then, once they have the ball, they wait. "Is it better to throw, punt or roll it to a teammate?", they think. Most of the time they won't take goal kicks as they should. Fullbacks should not take goal kicks, for this wastes their energy and keeps the goalie out of the game.

There is a shortage of good goalies of all ages, so if you have any interest at all in goalkeeping, give it a try! As "captain of the defense", you will guide all that goes on in the penalty area. Others depend on you. Although the ball seldom comes to you, you must always be ready for action.

53

Do everything you can to develop your footwork. You never know when you will be caught away from the penalty area, when you can't use your hands. Or, the coach may decide to place you in another position.

USING YOUR BODY

Although the ball is caught with the hands, the correct body position is also important. Some part of the body should be behind the hands, for safety.

The best goalies never take unnecessary chances. This is one way of making sure that the ball doesn't get loose. Ground balls should also be backed by the body, in the event of a bad bounce. Finally, you must fall to the ground to save some rolling balls.

Do this only when the ball is not in easy reach. The chest should always be behind the ball.

Once YOU HAVE CONFIDENCE

Goalies should have all the skills of strikers and defenders, plus several of their own. In addition to easy balls on the ground, and those that are sent right at you, there are others that must be saved. Practice in a sandpile or sawdust pit first, and get used to diving and falling on the ground. If you can dive and save balls, you will encourage the defense and bring support from the whole team.

Punching and deflecting balls not in easy reach will get you out of trouble when you are surrounded by players and cannot grab the ball with both hands.

Work with your fullbacks, so they understand what you want when you give the instructions in the game. It is also good practice to warm up each day with the other goalie on your team. You can help each other.

Finally, be fair to the coach and the team. If for some reason you think that goalkeeping is not for you, talk it over with the coach. In order to play it right, you must really want to play it. If you do, you'll enjoy it, and your confidence will grow each time you save a goal.

It's easy being a good sport when you have the trophy.
How can you be a good sport when you lose?
(Photo by Gary Weaver)

BEING A GOOD SPORT **11**

There is always a disappointment when you lose a game, especially a close one. The first thing you may want to do is get mad, and take it out on your opponents, teammates, the Referee, your coach, even your little sister!

There is nothing wrong with being disappointed, for it means you probably did your best and it wasn't quite good enough. Swallow your disappointment, give the winner a handshake, cheer up your teammates, and start thinking about your next game. That's good sportsmanship.

The game itself brings you plenty of good chances to be a good sport. If a player is injured, help him and give him encouragement. Pick up the ball for an opponent if it is his throw-in.

Chase down all out-of-bounds balls. Also, try
something like this: the next time your team
is scored upon, get your own players together
for a quick huddle. This will show everyone
you're still together after the disappointment
of a goal, and determined to get it back! If you
support the efforts of your teammates and sometimes give a friendly "nice try" to an opponent,
they will start treating you the same. With this
help, everyone does better, and you have
more fun.

Do you think this player won or lost? Does she seem to like the mud? (Photo by Bill Bowyer)

This is dangerous play against the player on the right.
Do you know what kind of free kick will result?
(Photo by Claudia Snider)

12
WHAT TO DO WHEN YOU'RE FOULED

Somewhere between 15 and 30 fouls will be called in your next game. Three or four may be against you, and some will be for you when you end up on the ground! Some will be ignored by the Referee, and still others will not be seen.

How many times have you seen players complain when they are fouled? They complain to the Referee, to their teammates, or to anyone who will listen. And, their biggest complaint is for the opponent who fouled, and we know he is planning to "get him back." Whatever the reasons for and circumstances of the foul, there are certain rules that good players in soccer follow:

1. After you've been fouled, even if you're on the ground, forget about the foul and start thinking of the free kick you're getting.

Where will it go? Who will take it? How do we get the game re-started right away? Is the kick indirect or direct?

2. Keep going with the ball, even if you've been

fouled. You may be better off with the ball than with the kick, and the "Ref" knows this.

3. Don't try to get sympathy by pretending you're injured. Everyone saw how hard you went down.

4. If you really think you're injured, don't try to be a hero by jumping up. It's better to wait and see how bad the injury really is.

13
KEEPING IN SHAPE

If you're serious enough about soccer to read this far, you probably want to know all about becoming the best player you can be. Although soccer is certainly a physically demanding game, your training and conditioning should not be much of a problem for you.

Your fitness will depend on how you train with your team for three or four hours each week. Every coach has his own ideas about training, and sometimes you may think he's being too hard on you. Remember the most important thing about training: the player who is "ready" will enjoy the game more, and is less likely to be injured. The following points are important. You may even want to talk them over with your coach.

1. Before you kick any ball or play any soccer you should "warm up". The amount will depend on the weather and how ready you are. If you've ridden your bike to practice in the warm weather, you will have less warming up to do than the player who has arrived by car in the cold. Jumping jacks, jogging in place, deep knee bends, and rope-skipping will all be good for you. Don't wear yourself out . . . just stretch those leg muscles.

2.   Do as many exercises as possible with the ball at your feet. The more time you spend with or near a ball, the better player you will become.

3.   After you've warmed up, try sprinting for short distances, then walk or jog, and sprint again. Sprint from unusual starting positions; like lying or sitting on the ground. Jogging for long distances won't do you any good. It just wears out those shoes. Now, do your sprinting with a ball at your feet.

4.   Play as many practice games as you can. This will get you conditioned to the stop and go of the real game.

You best exercise and conditioner is playing with the ball and doing things with it that you would in a game. Do it at game speed, and with your teammates. Don't wait for the coach to get you started. Always try something new to keep from getting bored in practice. Keep moving, and use the ball. When you do this, you won't have to worry about weights, or running up and down stairs, or circling the track 20 times. Soccer is fun, not drudgery.

64

The Referee will see most fouls, and will stop the game if he thinks you're injured. (Photo by John Becker)

65

Girls play soccer on the beach, too. (Photo by Gary Weaver)

14
GIRL'S SOCCER IS HERE

Girls, too, are moved by the energy of soccer. Since they enjoy freedom as much as anyone else, they are discovering soccer's joys. Many play in leagues, and have become coaches and referees, too.

The rules of girls' soccer are the same. Most referees allow girls to protect their chest with one or both arms. Everything else is the same, including the size of the ball and the length of a game. In fact, some boys and girls like playing soccer together.

The mistakes that girl players make are the same as boys, but are listed here because they seem to occur more in girls' play:

1. Girls are often afraid to head the ball. Try heading one that hangs from a rope on a tree.

Hint: Never wear hair clips. They are dangerous to you and to others.

2. Girls tend to lean back when they kick. Lean over the ball and follow through.
3. Girls favor one foot. Try leaving your kicking shoe at home for one practice a week. Watch what happens.

4. Girls turn away and jump when a ball is about to be kicked at them. Keep your feet on the ground whenever possible, and face the ball. You'll be able to see what's happening. The ball seldom hurts.

5. Girls would rather kick the ball away than trap it. If you are alone, first get the ball at your feet by trapping it.

6. Girls dislike being goalie, because they feel left out of the action. When you play in goal, come to the edge of the penalty area from time to time. You'll pick up long passes, feel more a part of the game, and learn more about what to do when the coach asks you to play in the field.

It should be remembered that all of these hints are for boys, too. Girls can learn alot from watching boys' games. And the boys can learn that girls always seem to be having fun at soccer, and that team spirit is there, win or lose!

Here's a girl (left) playing in a mixed league in Thousand Oaks, California.   (Photo by Fred Rasmussen)

*The Referee is careful that no one wears dangerous equip-
ment. Here he inspects for rings and watches before a game.
(Photo by John Rogers)*

15
WHAT THE REFEREE DOES, AND DOESN'T DO

When you are playing in a regular league, you will always have a referee for your game. He will sometimes be very young, sometimes older. There may even be two or more referees, and some are women. Whoever they are, they should be treated with respect and their decisions not questioned.

Remember that the Referee has studied the Laws of soccer. Although it may sometimes appear that the "Ref" is against you and your team, he is watching the game very closely, and is trying to be fair. If mistakes are made, remember that the Referee is part of the game, and all who are part of the game make errors.

Most Referees want to respect all players, but unfortunately it is not considered proper for them to congratulate players for good plays or for a victory. However, it is right for a player or his coach to thank the Referee after a game, and this shows good sportsmanship. The best act of sportsmanship is for the losing player to thank the Referee.

During the game, the players should not talk with the Referee. This distracts both player and Referee from doing their best. The Referee is to be treated as part of the field, and players should pretend not to notice him at all. The team captain, some players think, has a right to speak with the Referee whenever he wants. This is not true. The captain

is responsible for the good conduct of his teammates. He has been chosen because he sets a good example for others to follow.

If you want to know more about what is expected of the Referee, read chapter 4 again, for it tells about the laws which he must enforce.

THE REFEREE WILL:

1. Be polite. He expects you to be polite, too, both toward him and toward all other players.

2. Whistle only what he sees, not what he thinks he sees or what he may have heard.

3. Protect players from those who disobey the laws of the game.

4. See many things that you do not see.

5. Not listen to players or to others for advice.

6. Not explain why he called a foul. If he did this one time, he would always have to.

7. Not favor a team.

Pele was too busy playing soccer to have problems with
referees. Here, he waves "farewell" to his millons of fans
on his day of retirement. (Courtesy, Domicion Pinhero
and Pepsi-Cola)

Young players can learn from watching the professionals. Paul Child of the San Jose Earthquakes gives his autograph to hundreds of fans after every home game. Paul is a leading scorer in the North American Soccer League. (Photo courtesy of Tom Mertens, San Jose Earthquakes)

16
WOULD YOU LIKE TO WATCH THE PROS?

Nearly everyone who plays a sport likes to watch the professionals, just to see how they do it. If you are lucky to live near a city where professional soccer is played, you should go and watch some games. After a while you probably will have a favorite player, and you'll want to try some things he does.

It has been said before that the perfect soccer game has never been played. Did you know that in pro soccer one team loses possession of the ball to the other team more than 150 times? That's more than in basketball! Now maybe you won't feel too bad about your games. But before you think that you're ready for the pros, let's think about a few things they do well:

1. Experienced players run when they don't have the ball, always trying to make openings for passes and for their teammates with the ball.
2. Pros don't stop when they've been fouled. Only the whistle stops them.

3.   When two players are tackling for the ball, others will wait by at a close distance for a chance at the ball. They don't "gang up."
4.   Throw-ins are taken by the player nearest the ball.
5.   If an opening comes up, a player will move to that opening.
6.   Professional players do a lot of talking to each other.
7.   Even the best players have only a few good moves, but they do them well, and with either foot.
8.   When a player is about to be tackled, he goes in hard to keep the ball and to avoid injury.
9.   Free kicks and corner kicks are usually taken very soon after they are awarded.
10. If there is room, the ball is first controlled before it is kicked away.

You can learn from everyone who plays pro soccer. These players have no secrets. They do a lot of practicing and they keep in condition for their games. You can do the same.

Professionals have to be in top condition to play. Here is a scene from the 1974 World Cup. A player from Poland helps an injured player from Yugoslavia. (Photo by Horstmiller)

Kyle Rote is a friend of youth. He is respected by opposing teams, coaches, and all referees, and is an example in good sportsmanship. (Courtesy of Dallas Tornado)

78

17
AMERICAN SUCCESS
IN SOCCER KYLE ROTE, JR.

Soccer has just recently become popular in America. Countless thousands of players, sometimes without goalposts or uniforms, are playing the game in friendly competition and practice. Sometimes teams are mixed, with these games becoming very popular among boys and girls who play together.

With so many playing from the first years of school, new superstars will appear, and they will be American. The first of this generation is Kyle Rote Jr., a Texan who never kicked a soccer ball until he was almost 18 years old. At first he just wanted something to do when he was not playing football. He then found that soccer was fun and that he was challenged by having to use his feet. Six years after his first kick at the soccer ball, Kyle, whose father was a famous football player, was playing professional soccer for the Dallas Tornado.

Kyle also proved his ability by winning the "Superstars" competition on television, where he competed against other famous athletes in swimming, golf, bicycling, bowling, tennis, and others.

MORE SOCCER READING

There are three good soccer magazines in America.

SOCCER AMERICA Box 9393 Berkeley, California 94709.

This weekly magazine has many features about everything in the game, as well as news about soccer all over the U.S. and the world.

SOCCER MONTHLY The United States Soccer Federation, 4010 Empire State Building, New York, N.Y. 10001.

The official publication of the USSF. It has many articles of interest from around the world.

SOCCER WORLD Box 366 Mountain View, California 94040.

If you are really serious about soccer, this magazine will help you learn about tactics, conditioning, teamwork, skills, and coaching.

You may want to tell your coach or your parents about these books:

"Handbook for Youth Soccer", by D. J. Niotis. Available from Clyde Partin, Emory University, Atlanta, Georgia, 30322. This is a book for team organizers, and tells about how to start a league.

"Coaching Youth Soccer," by Neil Ingels, Jr. Distributed by **SOCCER FOR AMERICANS'** Box 836, Manhattan Beach, California 90266. This is an excellent book for any coach. Young players can learn a lot from it, too.

"So You'd Like to Know More about **SOCCER!** *A Guide for Parents"*, by Paul Harris. Available from **SOCCER FOR AMERICANS,** Box 836, Manhattan Beach, California 90266. Tells the soccer parents all about the game, and how he can help the youth player in his skills. Helps the parent learn a few skills, too.

"Teaching Soccer to Boys", by Alan Gibbon and John Cartwright. Available from Mr. Soccer, 14027 Floyd Road, Dallas, Texas 75240. An excellent book on teaching all the young player has to know about the game.

If you know someone who wants to know more about soccer refereeing . . .

"Fair or Foul? *The Complete Guide to Soccer Officiating in America",* by Paul and Larry Harris. Available from **SOCCER FOR AMERICANS,** Box 836, Manhattan Beach, California 90266. The book tells everything about the Referee and what he does and must do. Complete rules, with tests.

FILM

"The Master and His Method", distributed by Pepsi International Youth Soccer Program, PepsiCola, Purchase, New York 10577. There is nothing better in any sport than this series of films, featuring the great Pele. An instructional book is also available, with wall charts, too. Every player should see this series of films at least twice!

THE LANGUAGE OF SOCCER

Most of these terms are a part of your daily soccer activity. Some you should already know, but are listed here only because they are mentioned in the book. Others are not in the book, but are still important to your understanding.

Advantage
If the Referee feels that the whistle should not be blown, even though there has been a foul, he says, "Play on . . . advantage." He thinks that the player or team who was fouled is better off keeping the ball than getting a free kick.

Caution
If you continually disobey the game's laws, are unsportsmanlike, disagree with the Referee, or leave the field without the Referee's permission, you receive a caution (yellow card). If you do any one of these things again after receiving a yellow card, you will be ordered off the field by the Referee, and you cannot be replaced (red card).

Center
A pass that moves the ball from the outside to the center of the field.

Center Circle

The circle with the 10 yard radius at the center of the field.

Center Forward

The center player in the offensive attack, usually the one who scores a lot of goals. Sometimes called a "striker".

Charging

The maneuver of using a shoulder against an opponent's shoulder to gain an advantage. If the ball is within three feet (playing distance), charging is OK.

Club Linesmen

People who help the Referee by waving a flag when a ball goes out of bounds. They are on the touchline, and are appointed by the Referee only when no neutral linesman are present.

Corner Area

The arc at each corner of the field where corner kicks are taken.

Corner Flags

The four flags located in the four corners of the field. A ball hitting the flag and remaining in the field is in play. Do not remove the flag for corner kicks.

Corner Kick

A direct kick from the corner area, taken by the attacking team when the defense last played a ball over the goal line.

Cross

A Pass from one side of the field to the other, usually near the goal.

Dead Ball

A ball on the ground that is not rolling, but is playable.

Direct Kick
A free kick that may be kicked directly into the goal.

Dribbling
Controlling the ball by yourself on the ground, with the feet. Don't do too much dribbling, and never when it's easier to pass or shoot.

Drop Ball
A ball dropped by the Referee between two players. It happens when the Referee purposely stops the game. A drop ball will be given if play is stopped because of an injury or if the ball hit your girlfriend's dog.

Fair Charge (see Charging)
Fair charging of the goalkeeper is not usually allowed.

Forward
A "forward" player in the team formation. Sort of like a striker.

Free Kick
An unchallenged kick.

Fullbacks
The players who form the defense right in front of the goalie.

Goal Area
The area immediately in front of the goal, 20 x 6 yards in size.

Goalkeeper
Some players would rather be a goalie than spend a holiday at Disneyland. Others suddenly get sick when the coach asks them to stop a few kicks in goal. Are you like this?

Goal Kick

A kick taken from the goal area after the ball was last played by the attacking team over the goal line.

Goal Line

The line at the end of the field going from one touch-line to the other, including the part underneath the goalposts.

Halfbacks

The players who are the link between the fullbacks and the forwards. Often called "linkmen".

Half-Volley

The kick that is made on the short hop. Goalies sometimes drop-kick the ball. This is a half-volley.

Indirect Kick

A free kick that may not go directly into the goal. After it is kicked, someone else on either team must touch the ball for the goal to count.

Kickabout

An informal game of soccer, for exercise, ball control, and passing. You need four or more players for a kickabout.

Linesmen

They are referees with flags, and they signal for offsides and balls out of bounds. Also called "neutral linesmen."

Marking

As in "marking" your opponent. You stay very close so he can't get the ball when it is passed.

Obstruction

The act of deliberately placing yourself in the path of an opponent, with no attempt to play the ball.

Offside

Everybody's pest. Look at Law 11 on page 22.

Offside Position

You are usually in an offside position if there are not two opponents between you and their goal line. However, if you're not gaining anything by it, the Referee won't care.

Penal Offenses

The nine fouls that result in direct free kicks. They are shown on pages 24 and 25.

Outsides

The two forwards on the "outside", close to the touch-line. They usually take the corner kicks, and are the fastest players on the team, so they can outrun the fullbacks for the ball. Also called "wings" or "wingers."

Penalty Arc

The arc at the top of the penalty area. No player may be in this area when a penalty kick is being taken.

Penalty Area

The large area in front of the goal. It is 18 x 44 yards in size. The goalie may touch the ball in this area. All "direct" fouls by the defense in this area result in penalty kicks.

Penalty Kick

A "penalty" is taken 12 yards from the goal. It is given when one of the nine "direct" fouls occurs in the penalty area.

Referee

He "scores" the goals in his notebook that you "make." His job is not easy, but he likes it, and he tries to be fair.

Space

That's what you want to make in soccer. Space for yourself and for your teammates.

Striker
A player whose main job is to score goals.

Sweeper
A roving, dependable player who backs up the play of the defensemen.

Tackling
Taking the ball away from an opponent by using the feet. You can do it while standing or sliding.

Throw-in
The method of bringing the ball back into play after it has gone over the touchline. This is the easiest skill in soccer, yet often the most poorly done.

Touchline
The line on the side of the field where you take throw-ins. You may stand on the touchline to take your throw, if you wish.

Trapping
Getting the ball under control by using your body.

Volleying
Playing the ball with the foot before the ball reaches the ground.

Wall
A group of at least three defenders, in a position against a free kick near goal. The human "wall" must be 10 yards from the ball, or on the line between the goalposts.

Now that you know a little about soccer, you'll be ready to
try a few things with the ball, even when others are watching.
This player, with a brand new pair of shoes, is being watched
by coaches and players. He'll soon be playing on a team.
(Photo by Gary Weaver)

James